# YOUR KNOWLEDGE HAS

**Bibliographic information published by the German National Library:**

The German National Library lists this publication in the National Bibliography; detailed bibliographic data are available on the Internet at http://dnb.dnb.de .

**Imprint:**

Copyright © 2019 GRIN Verlag
Print and binding: Books on Demand GmbH, Norderstedt Germany
ISBN: 9783668987586

**This book at GRIN:**

https://www.grin.com/document/491439

**Gabriel Kabanda**

# Developments in Advanced Complexity Theory

GRIN Verlag

**GRIN - Your knowledge has value**

Since its foundation in 1998, GRIN has specialized in publishing academic texts by students, college teachers and other academics as e-book and printed book. The website www.grin.com is an ideal platform for presenting term papers, final papers, scientific essays, dissertations and specialist books.

**Visit us on the internet:**

http://www.grin.com/

http://www.facebook.com/grincom

http://www.twitter.com/grin_com

# ESSAY ON ADVANCED COMPLEXITY THEORY

Gabriel Kabanda

## ABSTRACT

The essay or review below describes or analyses the content, style and merit of the developments in Advanced Complexity Theory. Complex, self-organising, adaptive systems possess a kind of dynamism that makes them qualitatively different from static objects such as computer chips. Complex systems are more spontaneous, more disorderly, more alive than that. In the past three decades, chaos theory has shaken science to its foundations with the realisation that very simple dynamical systems can give rise to extraordinarily intricate behaviour. Chaos theory is the qualitative study of unstable, aperiodic behaviour in deterministic, non-linear, dynamical systems.Chaos / complexity scientists have identified a number of describing features of complex nonlinear systems. The main features of complex nonlinear systems are known to be "dynamic, nonlinear, chaotic, unpredictable, sensitive to initial conditions, open, self-organizing, feedback sensitive and adaptive". Two central aspects of chaos theory are the mathematical study of abstract dynamical systems and the application of these dynamical models to complex behaviour in actual experimental systems.There are three aspects of Chaos that relate to fractal patterns, bounded infinity, and unpredictability. Since the notions of nonlinearity incorporate both chaos theory in mathematics and complexity theory in science, an understanding of complexity theory might assist in the elucidation of chaotic concepts.

# Table of Contents

# 1. ANALYTICAL EXPOSITION

The essay or review below describes or analyses the content, style and merit of the developments in Advanced Complexity Theory. Complex, self-organising, adaptive systems possess a kind of dynamism that makes them qualitatively different from static objects such as computer chips. Complex systems are more spontaneous, more disorderly, more alive than that. In the past three decades, chaos theory has shaken science to its foundations with the realisation that very simple dynamical systems can give rise to extraordinarily intricate behaviour. The edge of chaos is the constantly shifting battle zone between stagnation and anarchy, the one place where a complex system can be spontaneous, adaptive, and alive (Waldrop, M.M, 1992). A provocative transition in dynamical systems is:

> Order ----> "Complexity" -----> Chaos.

Chaos theory is the qualitative study of unstable, aperiodic behaviour in deterministic, non-linear, dynamical systems (Kabanda, G., 2013). It is a specialised application of dynamical systems theory. Chaotic systems require impossible accuracy for useful prediction tasks. Chaos theory often seeks to understand the behaviour of a complex system by reconstructing its attractor, and knowing this attractor gives us qualitative understanding. Chaos theory includes theoretical hypotheses that assert relationships of qualitative (or topological) similarity between its abstract models and the actual systems it studies. Dynamics is used more as a source of qualitative insight than for making quantitative predictions. Its great value is its adaptability for constructing models of natural systems, which models can then be varied and analysed comparatively easily (Kabanda, G., 2013). Chaos theory is the quantitative study of dynamic non-linear system. Non-linear systems change with time and can demonstrate complex relationships between inputs and outputs due to reiterative feedback loops within the system. These systems are predictable but their behaviour is exquisitely sensitive to their starting point. Chaos is a sub-discipline of complexity. Complexity theory is the qualitative aspect drawing upon insights and metaphors that are derived from chaos theory.

Chaos / complexity scientists have identified a number of describing features of complex nonlinear systems. The main features of complex nonlinear systems are known to be "dynamic, nonlinear, chaotic, unpredictable, sensitive to initial conditions, open, self-organizing, feedback sensitive and adaptive" (Larsen-Freeman, 1997, p. 142). A numerical simulation of the behaviour of the system may reveal a period-doubling cascade. One should then obtain the scaling relations by examining the sequence of birfucation points, identify the relevant symmetries of the situation, and test the generality of these features by exploring other similar maps. This theory gives us understanding by showing us the mechanism responsible for unpredictable behaviour, but these are not causal processes. It is always appropriate to see understanding as providing knowledge of underlying causes. Chaos theory then relies heavily on digital computers. Two central aspects of chaos theory are the mathematical study of abstract dynamical systems and the application of these dynamical models to complex behaviour in actual experimental systems. Specific manifestations of chaotic solutions had to wait for the arrival of powerful computers with which to calculate the long-time histories necessary to observe and measure chaotic behaviour.

Chaos / complexity theory is concerned with the behavior of dynamic systems, i.e., the systems that change in time. The study of chaos (the randomness generated by complex systems) is a study of process and becoming, rather than state and being. Dynamic systems move through space / time, following a path called an attractor, i.e., the state or pattern that a dynamic system is attracted to (Larsen-Freeman, 2002). Chaos / complexity theory focuses on complex systems. To Larsen-Freeman (1997), systems are complex for two reasons. First, they often include a large number of components, and second, the behavior of complex systems is more than a product of the behavior of its individual components.The outcome of a complex system emerges from the interactions of its components; it is not built in any one component. As such, the interactions (connectivities) amongst the components in the system are the essential building blocks of the unpredictable structures that may emerge in the future.

Logistic functions are generally expressed as the function: $x_{k+1} = \lambda x_k(1 - x_k)$ and are used to display patterns associated with population growth and decline, where the minimum value is zero and the maximum possible size is one (1). The constant $\lambda$ is used a parameter to account for different species. Values less than zero (0) and greater than 1, when iterated, are going to move toward (negative) infinity, thus the scale to display should focus mainly between $x = 0$ and 1. The line $y = x$ is used as a reference point for each iteration, since the resulting y becomes the new x. The process of iteration displays a relationship between the initial seed and its ensuing values for the function (Smitherman, S., 2014, p.5).There are three specific ideas that relate to the classroom and which draw on conceptual understandings associated with nonlinear dynamics: fractal patterns, bounded infinity, and unpredictability. These ideas incorporate various perspectives of chaos theory that exhibit patterns of nonlinearity (Smitherman, S., 2014, p.5).
There are three aspects of Chaos that relate to fractal patterns, bounded infinity, and unpredictability (Smitherman, S., 2014, p.6):

i.   Fractal Patterns
    Fractals are patterns of self-similarity that are generated using iterated functions. The word fractal is a way to describe geometric patterns that do not become more simplified (reduced) as one zooms in or out. According to Smithernan (2014, p.6), patterns of behavior in a classroom can relate to these fractal patterns. Still others are chaotic, like the behavior of students that are performed each day in the classroom. These fractaled patterns display dynamic relations that occur within a classroom among teachers, students, subject material and the classroom environment. By relating conversations in the classroom to fractal patterns, teachers can embrace a rich metaphor as a picture of what is occurring. The initial seed will have an impact on what conversation will ensue, the format of the discussion will affect the type of interaction, and the patterns of the resulting conversation may in fact display differing "orbits."

ii.  Bounded Infinity
    Consider all the numbers that exist on a number line between the integers of zero and one. That is one example of a bounded set of an infinite amount of members. Teachers can connect to this notion of bounded infinity in their classrooms. A teacher may be restricted (bounded) by the national initiatives, state mandates, district criteria, school instructions, and curricular concerns, but within these boundaries are infinite possibilities. The potential relationships between teacher and students, among students, and how a teacher chooses to implement the subject material are boundless. This grants freedom to the teacher to not feel constricted by the limits that are imposed by outside sources but rather to be creative within them (Smitherman, S., 2014, p.9.

iii. Unpredictability

Chaos theory incorporates the notion that sensitive dependence to initial conditions is an important component needed to generate chaotic behaviors. Small variations in conditions may lead to large differences in nonlinear dynamical systems. Non-linear, open systems are divergent and generative, not closed and limited. An immediate consequence of sensitive dependence in any system is the impossibility of making perfect predictions, or even mediocre predictions sufficiently far into the future. Predicting becomes problematic beyond certain ranges of time (Smitherman, S., 2014, p.10).

Since the notions of nonlinearity incorporate both chaos theory in mathematics and complexity theory in science, an understanding of complexity theory might assist in the elucidation of chaotic concepts. The two areas are not mutually exclusive and should not be interpreted as such (Smitherman, S., 2014, p.13). While chaos theory is located within mathematics, complexity theory situates itself in science. The field of complex systems cuts across all traditional disciplines of science, as well as engineering, management, and medicine. It focuses on certain questions about parts, wholes and relationships. Complexity theory is an emerging field in which scientists seek patterns and relationships within systems. Rather than looking to cause and effect relations, complexity theorists seek to explicate how systems function to rely upon feedback loops (reiteration, recursion, reciprocity) so as to (re)frame themselves and thus continue to develop, progress, and emerge (Smitherman, S., 2014, p.16).

Complex non-linear dynamic systems, as illustrated by Figure 1 below, can be:

◆ dynamic: the behaviour of the system (e.g. classroom) as a whole arises from the interaction of its components.
◆ complex: any learning situation is influenced by many factors (teaching/learning characteristics, interaction patterns, methods, materials, time, etc.)
◆ nonlinear: learners learn in "jumps".

**Figure 1: Chaotic behavior**

The initial condition x gives after time t a point f'x. If x is replaced by x+□x, then f'x is replaced by f'x+□ f'x , and □ f'x = (□ f'x/□ x). □ x grows exponentially with time t, we say that we have sensitive dependence on initial condition. More precisely, we have sensitive dependence on initial condition if the matrix of partial derivatives □ f'x/□ x has norm growing exponentially with t.

An attractor is the set on which the point P, representing the system of interest, is moving at large times (i.e. after so-called transients have died out) (Ruelle, D., 1991). For this definition to make sense it is important that the external forces acting on the system be time independent (otherwise we could get the point P to move in any way we like). It is also important that we consider dissipative systems (viscous fluids dissipate energy by self-friction). Dissipation is the reason transients die out. Strange attractors look strange in that they are not smooth curves or surfaces but have "non-integer dimension", i.e. they are fractal objects. The motion on a strange attractor has sensitive dependence on initial condition. What we now call **chaos** is a time evolution with sensitive dependence on initial condition. The motion on a strange attractor is thus chaotic (Kabanda, G., 2013).

The more general definition of an attractor is a set of points or states in state space to which trajectories within some volume of state space converge asymptotically over time (Kauffmann, S.A, 1993). Many but not all dynamical systems have attractors. Among those which do not are the classical Hamiltonian systems of physics, exemplified by the frictionless pendulum. If released at any defined position and initial velocity, the pendulum swings on a periodic, closed orbit in its state space without loss of energy. If displaced to a slightly larger or smaller orbit by a perturbation, the pendulum follows a different closed, periodic orbit in its state space, with a slightly different energy. Each obit is neutrally stable, for the system will remain in any orbit once placed there. No orbit drains a basin of attraction. The existence of attractors requires some form of driving and friction which prevents conservation of energy within the system itself. Thus, in addition to simple steady states, continuous dynamical systems may admit of more complex attractors.

The limit cycle is one type of an attractor where the system flows around in a loop repeatedly. Strange or chaotic attractors exist (Lorenz, E.N., 1963; Ruelle, D., 1979; Grassberger, P. and Procaccia, I., 1983; Mayer-Kress, G., 1986). In such a dynamical system, which might be ten-dimensional, the flow might, for example, bring all trajectories onto a two-dimensional attractor a bit like a Moebius strip with a pleat or some other folded form. The interesting property of such attractors is that, if the system is released from two points on the attractor which are arbitrarily close to each other, the subsequent trajectories remain on the attractor surface but diverge away from each other. The dimensionality of a strange attractor is often not an integer. Rather it is natural to define a fractal dimension (Mandelbrot, B., 1977) for the attractor, which might be 2.3 for an attractor which occupies more than two but fewer than three dimensions in the 100-dimensional space (Packard et al, 1980; Mayer-Kress, G., 1986). Such fractal attractors are already being found in biological systems - for example, in cardiac and neural electrical activity patterns (Holden, A.V., 1986, Mackey, M.C., and Glass, L.,1988).

Deng, Z., and Hioe, F.T. (1985) presented a result which showed the transitions from chaos to order and again to chaos as the coupling parameter between two nonlinearly coupled oscillators of a Hamiltonian system is varied continuously from - ∞ to +∞. He showed that there is no general correspondence between the classical chaotic motion and the Gaussian-orthogonal-ensemble distributions of the energy-level fluctuations of the corresponding quantum system.

Current models of neural nets, which may use a sigmoidal output response from the neuron to the input activity level rather than an all-or-none output from the neuron (Hinton et al., 1984; Hinton, G.E., and Sejnowski, T.J., 1986). Hinton et al., 1986; Hopfield et al, 1986a, 1986b; Grossberg, 1987), often seek to model pattern-recognition capacities and associative memories by these parallel-processing networks in terms of attractors of such networks (Hopfield, J.J., 1982a, 1982b; Toulouse et al., 1986). For example the attractors might be thought of either as memories held by the neural network or as concepts. Then such networks are naturally content-addressable, i.e. if released in the basin of attraction of a specific memory or concept, the system will flow under the dynamics of the network to that attractor.

**Decidability**
Many decision problems associated with the class of recursive functions are undecidable. To show that a decision problem is undecidable may be achieved through relating it in an appropriate way to another problem that is already undecidable, a process called reducing one decision problem to another. The idea of *computability* is closely related to that of *decidability*.

Informally, the problem of determining whether a designated property holds for arbitrarily chosen objects is said to be decidable if there is an effective procedure for making the required decision. Formally, such a decision problem is defined to be recursively decidable if the number-theoretic relation corresponding to the property in question is recursive. Undecidability is most commonly established by the method of reduction, which consists in showing that a decision procedure for the problem at hand would provide a decision procedure for some problem already known to be undecidable. Rice's theorem uses this approach   to show that many simple problems concerning recursive functions are undecidable.

7

**Rice's Theorem:**
Let P be any proper nonempty subset of the one-variable recursive functions.
$A = \{X\square \ y_x \square \ P\}$.     Then the set A is not recursive.

According to Rice's Theorem, there can be no algorithmic procedure for determining, on the basis of an index alone, whether a recursive function satisfies a given nontrivial property. One of the most useful reduction techniques is that known as many-one reduction. A set B is said to be many-one reducible to a set A if there is a total recursive function that maps members of B into members of A and nonmembers of B into nonmembers of A. The existence of such a function implies that the problem of determining membership in A must be undecidable whenever  the problem of determining membership of B is undecidable. This fact provides a way of establishing the undecidability of many interesting problems.

*Chaotic Systems*
The behaviour of a disordered system could be due to random noise or low-dimensional deterministic but chaotic dynamics. This theory that describes and justifies the procedure for the reconstruction of a system's dynamics draws heavily on differential topology.

The time series described by
$$y(t) = \sin(t) + \sin(\square \ 2t)$$
gives a signal that is composed of two modes, and the apparent disorder arises because the periods of the modes are incommensurate, i.e. their ratio is irrational. This is referred to as quasiperiodicity.

The logistic map
$$x_{n+1} = \square \ x_n(1 \text{-} x_n)$$
generates a string of values of $X_n$ given a starting value $X_o$. The time series is disordered, even though the governing equation is very simple. This is an example of a chaotic system, one that is governed by a low-dimensional set of equations but that has a broad-band spectrum. The logistic map is one of the simplest and most mathematically tractable examples of a chaotic system.

The Lorenz system gives an approximation to the Navier-Stokes equation for a convection system, one of the first sets of differential equations found to show a chaotic behaviour. The system consists of three non-linear first-order ordinary differential equations:
$$x' = \square \ (y - x)$$
$$y' = \square \ x - y \ \text{-} xz$$
$$z' = \text{-}\square \ z + xy$$

There are three degrees of freedom for the Lorenz system, showing that the system evolution takes place on a well-defined subset of three-dimensional space (an "attractor") (Gershenfeld, N., 1988). An attractor is a set of points or states in state space to which trajectories within some volume of state space converge asymptotically over time (Kauffman, S.A., 1993).

*Chaos and Noise*
It is important to distinguish between random noise and deterministic chaos. Deterministic chaos occurs in a low-dimensional space, while random noise does not.

## Time Delay

Information theory can be used to quantify the relation between the time delay and the amount of information available from a measurement, as is the case in message communication in signalling systems. The information entropy of a system that has a meter to indicate n different values $v_1, v_2, .., v_n$ with observed probabilities $P(v_1), P(v_2), ..., P(v_n)$, is defined by:

$$I = - \sum_i P(v_i) \log_2 P(v_i)$$

The function defined above is continuous in the probabilities and, if all the probabilities are equal it is a monotonically increasing function of n. If a choice can be broken down into successive sub-choices, then I should be a weighted sum of the entropies of the sub-choices. I provides a measure of the amount of information that is gained by a measurement of v. If a measurement has a probability of either one or zero then I equals zero, and the entropy is maximized by the greatest uncertainty ($P = \frac{1}{2}$). The entropy can be naturally defined for continuous quantities:

$$I = - \int P(s) \log_2 P(s) ds.$$

Our goal is to be able to predict information about the next measurement in the next time delay or interval.

## The Embedding Dimension

A manifold is a generalised notion of a surface that allows it to be described without reference to an external co-ordinate system. A simple two-dimensional manifold can be obviously embedded into a two dimensional real space.

## Analysing the Dynamics

A hydrodynamic system has infinitely many degrees of freedom, yet just beyond the onset of convection it can act as a very low dimensional system. The Center Manifold theorem guarantees that the linearization of a dynamical system accurately reflects the full non-linear dynamics. In the local linearization there will be stable, unstable, and neutrally stable degrees of freedom. Ultimately, the unstable degrees of freedom will diverge until they reach a bound, the table degrees will exponentially vanish, and so the dynamics will collapse down onto the neutral degrees of freedom ("center manifold"). The center manifold, if it exists, will frequently have fewer dimensions than the full system, and so the system will behave as if it had only this reduced number of degrees of freedom. A more complicated possibility is for the stable and unstable manifolds to cross; a situation related which is related to chaos.

The Lorenz attractor comes from a three-dimensional system, yet its correlation dimension of 2.05 is distinctly less than three. This difference suggests that a full three-dimensional plot of the evolution of the Lorenz system, contains redundant information about the flow. The Poincare section is a standard technique, generally applied to near-periodic systems, that is used to dissect the flow and produce a more lucid representation. This section is formed by taking a surface transverse to the flow, and then plotting the intersections of the flow with the surface. The Poincare section replaces the continuous time dynamical system with a map. This map may have a much simpler structure than was obvious from the original system, and serve as a useful step and guide for further analysis.

*Lyapunov Exponents*

The divergence of nearby trajectories underlies the sensitive dependence on initial conditions in a strange attractor. The Lyapunov exponents quantify the relationship between nearby trajectories, and they will provide another indicator of the presence of chaos. Consider the growth of an arbitrary perturbation dx about a point x. The growth rate of this perturbation will be exponential, with the rates locally given by the eigenvalues of the Jacobian matrix:

$$dx/dt = f(x)$$
$$d(x + \delta x)/dt = f(x + \delta x)$$
$$df/dt + (d/dt)\delta x \approx f(x) + (D_x f)\delta x$$

Each of the eigenvectors of the Jacobian matrix $D_x f$ will locally grow at a rate $e^{\lambda_i t}$, where the $\lambda_i$ 's are the eigenvalues of the matrix. Taking the flow to be $u_t$, the growth of dx is given by the Jacobian, $T_x^t$ of the flow:

$$\delta x(t) = T_x^t \, \delta x(0) = (D_x u_t) \, \delta x(0)$$

The Lyapunov exponents are given by the asymptotic growth rate of the eigenvalue of $T_x^t$:

$$\{\lambda\} = \lim_{t \to \infty} \| T_x^t \| / t$$

This definition is easily extended to discrete time systems, where the flow $u_t$ is replaced by the nth iterate of the map $u_n$. $T_x^n$ is defined to be the Jacobian of $u_n$, and the chain rule allows this to be written as the product of the derivatives of the map at the points along the trajectory:

$$T_x^n = D_{x0}u^n$$
$$= D_{x0}(u...u)$$
$$= (D_{xn-1}u)...(D_{x1}u)(D_{x0}u)$$

A dynamical system may have some positive exponents, corresponding to directions associated with chaotic stretching, some negative ones, corresponding to directions of contraction, and some zero ones, corresponding to directions in which trajectories at most converge or diverge at a rate slower than exponential; the distribution of the signs of the exponents is itself a useful description of the nature of the dynamics. The positive exponents are traditionally ordered as $\lambda_1 \geq \lambda_2 \geq \lambda_3 ,..., \geq \lambda_n$.

Weak turbulence is the deterministic chaos associated with the detection of chaos. The theory given above offers little insight into strong turbulence, which is the disorder of, for example, the fully-developed turbulence of a high Reynold's number fluid flow. The interactions of the eddies and vortices in such flows are certainly governed by deterministic rules.

## 2. CRITICAL CONTEXT:

The major focus of complexity theory is on resources such as time and space needed to solve computational problems. However, there are some problems that are computable in principle which resist all attempts to compute them in a reasonable amount of time (Terwijn, S.A., 2017, p.1). Complexity theory is also the home of one of the most fundamental open problems in mathematics, namely the famous NP versus P problem.

Given a set $\Sigma$, the set of all finite strings of elements from $\Sigma$ is denoted by $\Sigma*$. (This set is also referred to as the set of all words over the alphabet $\Sigma$.) The $*$-operator is called Kleene star. We usually work over the set of finite binary strings $\{0, 1\}*$, that can be interpreted as binary representations of the natural numbers N. The length of a string x is denoted by $|x|$, and $\{0, 1\}n$ denotes the set of strings of length n. The concatenation of strings x and y is denoted by $x^\wedge y$ or simply by xy (Terwijn, S.A., 2017, p.1)

Spielman, D.A. (2001) defines the following inclusive classes list for advanced complexity as shown on Table 1 below:

**Table 1: Inclusive Classes list (Source: Spielman, D.A., 2001, p.1-2)**

| Class | Complete Problem | Reduction |
|-------|-----------------|-----------|
| EXPTIME | NREGEXP | $\leq P$ |
| PSPACE | TQBF | $\leq P$ |
| NP | 3SAT | $\leq P$ |
| P | CVP | $\leq L$ |
| NL | STCONN | $\leq L$ |
| L | ISPATH | $\leq L$ |

It is noted from the above table that $P \subset BPP \subset PSPACE$.

Objects such as formulas and Turing machines that can be coded using strings from $\{0, 1\}*$ are routinely handled as such. Subsets $A \subseteq \{0, 1\}*$ are variously called *set*, *problem* (in case we think of it as a decision problem, namely to decide for a given element x whether $x \in A$), or *language*. (Terwijn, S.A., 2017, p.1). We often identify a set $A$ with its characteristic sequence, i.e. we write $A(x) = 1$ if $x \in A$ and $A(x) = 0$ otherwise. For a given set $A$, $A$ denotes the complement of A, and $\bar{A}$ x denotes the finite set $A \cap \{0 \ldots x\}$, or equivalently, the finite string $A(0)A(1)\ldots A(x)$ (Terwijn, S.A., 2017, p.2).

For a given class $C$ of sets, *co-C* denotes the class $A : A \in C$ of all sets whose complement is in C. $|A|$ denotes the cardinality of A.

In complexity theory Turing machines are allowed to have any finite number of tapes. Given a Turing machine M and an input x, we use the notation $M(x) \downarrow$ to denote that the computation of M on x halts in a finite number of steps, and we write $M(x)\uparrow$ if this is not the case. A set or a function is computable if there is a Turing machine computing it.

Given a computable set A and a machine M that computes A, we also say that M recognizes A, or that M accepts A. A Turing machine is nondeterministic if at any computation step, there is a set of next possible states, rather than a single next state as in a deterministic computation (Terwijn, S.A., 2017, p.2).

On any given input, there is a set of possible computation paths, rather than a single one. By definition, a nondeterministic Turing machine accepts an input when some computation path accepts it (Terwijn, S.A., 2017, p.2). We will often use the existence of universal Turing machines, that is, the existence of a machine M with two arguments such that for any Turing machine M' there exists i ∈ N (thought of as a code for M') such that
$M(i, x) = M'(x)$ for any x.

Here $M(i, x)$ is defined as $M(hi, xi)$. This means that there is an computable list $\{M_i\}i \in N$ of all Turing machines (Terwijn, S.A., 2017, p.3).

We use the following common notation to compare the asymptotic behavior of functions on N. The phrase "for almost all n ∈ N" means "for all n except perhaps finitely many".

$f \in O(g)$ if there is a constant c ∈ N such that for almost all n we have $f(n) \leq cg(n)$.

The Big-O notation is often used to introduce constants without having to name them: $f \in O(1)$ means that f is bounded by a constant. For example, $g(n) \leq n$. $O(1)$ means that g is at most of polynomial growth. Big O and small o also have a dual notation, denoted with omegas(Terwijn, S.A., 2017, p.3) :

$f \in \omega(g)$ if for every constant c ∈ N there are infinitely many n such that $f(n) > cg(n)$.

$f \in \Omega(g)$ if there is a real constant r > 0 such that for infinitely many n, $f(n) > rg(n)$

A literal is a Boolean variable or the negation thereof. For a literal x its negation is denoted by $\bar{x}$. A clause is a disjunction of literals. Clauses are often denoted using set notation, so the set of literals $\{x_1, \ldots, x_k\}$ denotes the clause $x_1 V . . Vx_k$. denotes the empty clause, and stands for false. A Boolean formula is in conjunctive normal form (CNF) if it is a conjunction of clauses. A formula is in disjunctive normal form (DNF) if it is a disjunction of conjunctions of literals (Terwijn, S.A., 2017, p.4) :

The order (cardinality) of $(Z/nZ)*$is denoted by $\phi(n)$. The function $\phi$ is called the Euler phi function. For p prime we have $\phi(p) = p - 1$, as is easily seen from the definition of $(Z/pZ)*$. Theorem on (Euler) x:
$\phi(n) \equiv 1$ mod n for all x and n with $\gcd(x, n) = 1$.

According to Terwijn (2017, p.6), it is customary to measure the complexity of computations in the size of the input, which is usually its length when represented as a binary string. This means in particular that the size of a number n ∈ N is of order log n. (Unless stated otherwise, log is always to the base 2.) We only want to consider resource bounds that are reasonable in the following sense.

❖ t : N → N is time constructible if there is a Turing machine which on every input of length n halts in precisely t(n) steps.
❖ s : N → N is space constructible if there is a Turing machine that on every input of length n halts in a configuration with exactly s(n) non?blank tape cells and that used no other cells during the computation.

Given such constructible resource bounds we define the following classes (Terwijn, S.A., 2017, p.7) :
❖ TIME(t) is the class of all sets that are accepted by a Turing machine within running time t(n) for all inputs of length n.
❖ NTIME(t) is defined as TIME(t), but now with nondeterministic Turing machines.
❖ SPACE(s) is the class of all sets that are accepted by a Turing machine using space at most s(n) for all inputs of length n.
❖ NSPACE(s) is defined as SPACE(s), but now with nondeterministic Turing machines.

Terwijn (2017, p.7) defines the following inclusions between classes:
❖ TIME(t) ⊆ NTIME(t), SPACE(s) ⊆ NSPACE(s).
❖ TIME(t) ⊆ SPACE(t), NTIME(t) ⊆ NSPACE(t). This holds because a machine cannot use more space than time.
❖ SPACE(c · s) ⊆ SPACE(s) for any c ∈ N. This result is called the tape compression theorem. The idea of the proof is to increase the tape alphabet by introducing a symbol for every block of length c. Idem for
❖ NSPACE. The result means that we can work with O(s) rather than s
❖ in the future.
❖ TIME(c · t) ⊆ TIME(t) for any c ∈ N and t with n ∈ o(t), i.e. such that ∀r > 0∀
❖ NTIME(t) ⊆ SPACE(t). Reuse space! We only need to keep a counter of length t for the current path. This gives NTIME(t) ⊆ SPACE(2t) = SPACE(t).
❖ NSPACE(s) ⊆ SPACE($s^2$).

One of the central themes in complexity theory is the difference between determinism and nondeterminism, and the tradeoff between time and space. This translates into the most prominent questions P ≠ NP and P ≠ PSPACE.

P is often identified with the class of problems that are solvable in "reasonable" time, although it may of course depend on the context what one finds reasonable. In contrast, NP corresponds to the class of problems of which it may be hard to find solutions, but of which one can efficiently check whether a candidate solution really is one. Because it does seem not very useful if one cannot even check whether a solution is correct, one could with a bit of exaggeration say that NP is the largest class of problems that one would be interested in knowing the answers to. (Terwijn, S.A., 2017, p.13) :

Consider nondeterministic Turing machines M whose computation trees are full binary trees, and in which every computation path has the same length. Given a set L and a machine M that is supposed to compute L, and an input x, the error probability is the ratio of the number of paths giving the wrong answer and the total number of paths. When thinking of Turing machines in this way we speak also of probabilistic Turing machines.

## 3. INTEGRATIVE CONCLUSION

Complexity does not mean the same as complicated. A complicated system can be broken into parts, like an airplane. In complex systems, there are no parts, only patterns, that we recognize in that moment. The patterns mean something in relation to the entire whole, and the patterns inform what that whole might be (Ruelle, D., 1991). Systems thinking emerged in science in the 1930s where scientists looked to relationships and properties of systems, recognizing that a systems approach becomes necessary. In the next decade a group of scholars from different fields interested in the "mind" entered into a series of conversations (Smitherman, S., 2014, p.15).

Three important concepts in this paper include the notions that time is irreversible; there is order among chaos; and, systems can be perceived as dissipative structures. Each concept is significant because each differs from contemporary scientific thought. Dissipative structures are described as systems that may transform into new patterns when caught in far-from-equilibrium conditions. Von Neumann created a simple machine that would display patterns of cellular automata that undergo specific properties as a way to show random patterns emerging out of simple rules. Each cellular automaton is an on/off switch that changes according to the conditions of its neighbors' states. The grid of cellular automata displays the states of each automaton as they are updated by the conditions of the neighboring cells (Smitherman, S., 2014, p.23). According to Smitherman (2014, p.26), Chaos Theory has many components that are interconnected, and these include the following:

A. Orbit Analysis (orbits, critical points, periodic points, period doubling, strange attractors)
B. Initial Conditions and Sensitive Dependence
C. Recursion, Iteration, Feedback
D. Complex Numbers and Functions
E. Logistic Equations
F. Mandelbrot set and Julia sets

Two central aspects of chaos theory are the mathematical study of abstract dynamical systems and the application of these dynamical models to complex behaviour in actual experimental systems. An attractor is a set of points or states in state space to which trajectories within some volume of state space converge asymptotically over time (Kauffman, S. The more general definition of an attractor is a set of points or states in state space to which trajectories within some volume of state space converge asymptotically over time (Kauffmann, S. complex: any learning situation is influenced by many factors (teaching/learning characteristics, interaction patterns, methods, materials, time, etc. Information theory can be used to quantify the relation between the time delay and the amount of information available from a measurement, as is the case in message communication in signalling systems. Chaos / complexity theory focuses on complex systems. P is often identified with the class of problems that are solvable in "reasonable" time, although it may of course depend on the context what one finds reasonable. A hydrodynamic system has infinitely many degrees of freedom, yet just beyond the onset of convection it can act as a very low dimensional system. This holds because a machine cannot use more space than time.

# REFERENCES

DENG, Z., and Hioe, F.T., (1985). "Chaos-Order-Chaos Transitions in a two-dimensional Hamiltonian System", in Physical Review Letters, Volume 55, Number 15, 7 October 1985.

GERSHENFELD, N., (1988). "An Experimentalist's introduction to the observation of dynamical systems", in Directions of Chaos, Hao Bai-lin edition, World Scientific, 1988.

GRASSBERGER, P. and Procacia, I., (1983). "Measuring the strangeness of strange attractors", in Physica 9D, pp189, 1983.

HINTON, G.E. and Sejnowski, T.J., (1986). "Learning and relearning in Boltzmann machines", Report CMU-CS-86-004, Department of Computer Science, Carnegie-Mellon University, Pittsburg 1986.

HINTON, G.E., Sejnowski, T., and Ackley, D., (1984). "Boltzmann machines: Constraint satisfaction networks that learn", Report CMU-CS-84-119, Department of Computer Science, Carnegie-Mellon University, Pittsburg, 1984.

HOLDEN, A.V., (1986). Chaos, Princeton, New Jersey: Princeton University Press, 1986.

HOPFIELD, J.J.,(1982). "Neural networks and physical systems with emergent collective computational abilities", in Proceedings of Natural Academy Science USA, Volume 79, pp2554, 1982a.

HOPFIELD, J.J., (1982). "Neural networks and physical systems with emergent collective computational abilities", in Proceedings of Natural Academy Science USA, Volume 83, pp1847, 1982b.

HOPFIELD, J.J., and Tank, D.W., (1986). "Computing with neural circuits: A model", in Science, Volume 233, pp625, 1986a.

HOPFIELD, J.J., and Tank, D.W., (1986). " Collective computation with continuous variables", in *Disordered Systems and Biological Organization*, E. Bienenstock edition. New York: Springer, Volume 20, 1986b.

KABANDA, G., (2013). "African context for technological futures for digital learning and the endogenous growth of a knowledge economy ", Basic Journal of Engineering Innovation (BRJENG), Volume 1(2), April 2013, pages 32-52, to http://basicresearchjournals.org/engineering/PDF/Kabanda.pdf

KAUFFMAN, S.A., (1993). The origins of order: selg-organization and selection in evolution, New York: Oxford University Press, 1993.

LARSEN-FREEMAN, D., (1997). Chaos/complexity science and second language acquisition. Applied Linguistics, 18(2), 141-165.

LARSEN-FREEMAN, D. (2002). Language acquisition and language use from a chaos / complexity theory perspective. In C. Kramsch (Ed.), Language acquisition and socialization (pp.33-46). London: Continuum International Publishing Group.

LORENZ, E.N., (1963). "Deterministic nonperiodic flow", in Journal of Atmospheric Science, pp130, Volume 20, 1963.

MACKEY, M.C., and Glass, L.,(1988). From clocks to Chaos: The Rhythm of Life, Princeton, New Jersey: Princeton University Press, 1988.

MANDELBROT, B., (1977). The Fractal Geometry of Nature, San Francisco: Freeman, 1977.

MAYER-KRESS, G., (1986). Dimensions and Entropies in Chaotic Systems: Quantification of Complex Behaviour, Berlin: Springer-Verlag, 1986.

PACKARD, N.H., and Crutchfield, J.P., et al., "Geometry from a time series", in Physical Review Letters Volume 45, pp712, 1980.

RUELLE, D., (1979). "Sensitive dependence on initial condition and turbulent behaviour of dynamical systems", in Annuls of New York Academy of Science, Volume 316, pp408, 1979.
RUELLE, D. (1991). Chance and Chaos, New Jersey, Princeton University Press, 1991.

SMITHERMAN, S., (2014). Chaos and Complexity Theories: Creating Holes and Wholes in Curriculum, The Chaos and Complexity Theories SIG at the AERA Annual Meeting, San Diego, CA, on Thursday, April 15, 2004.

SPIELMAN, D.A., (2001). Advanced Complexity Theory, Lecture Notes for Course 18.405J/6.841J, MIT, February, 2001.

TERWIJN, S.A., (2017). Complexity Theory Course Notes, Radboud University Nijmegen, The Netherlands, December 2017.

TOULOUSE, G., Dehaene, S., and Changeux, J.P., "Spin-glass model of learning by selection", in Proceedings of Natural Academy of Sciences USA, Volume 83, pp1695, 1986.

WALDROP, M.M., (1992). Complexity: The emerging science at the edge of order and chaos: Touchestone, New York, 1992.

# YOUR KNOWLEDGE HAS VALUE

- We will publish your bachelor's and master's thesis, essays and papers

- Your own eBook and book - sold worldwide in all relevant shops

- Earn money with each sale

Upload your text at www.GRIN.com
and publish for free